Introduction

If there is something that has fascinated me since childhood, are the dinosaurs. What child does not dream, bad or good, with those huge monsters that lurk among the woods and that emit roars showing their sharp teeth. Movies like Jurassic Park keep that magic and terror latent transport us to the past reminding us that the world was once dominated by creatures that, no longer exist. We emphasize the ferocity of some of these reptiles and do little to show how peaceful many of them were, without a doubt, the big teeth and the cold look of the bloodthirsty hunter sells the product better.

Prehistory had a whole range of giants, gentle and fierce, but there were also those little ones with the same behavior.

I remember that I recently gave a nephew an amber, a fossil resin of almost 80 million years, that had a mosquito and a spider trapped inside.

- "What uncle, how small were the insects at that time?" - He was surprised.

Of course, there were all sizes, at different times and in different shapes.

Very little is really known about prehistory, much of what we know or presume, we have received it from film or television. If I asked anyone in the streets of Peru, where the dinosaurs lived, surely the vast majority would tell me that in the United States.

Many people ignore that Peru is one of the countries with more paleontological wealth worldwide, these lands contains all ages and a diversity of animals that, even, are not classified by paleontology, that science that deals with rebuilding, about the base of remains, almost always petrified or embedded in rocks, the physiological and morphological characteristics of the organisms of the past. It also serves to know the origin of each living species and its relationship with missing organisms. Living beings exist for millions of years, long before the dinosaurs or the human being stepped on the face of the earth.

Science tells us that at the beginning our planet was inhabited by unicellular, microorganisms that consisted of a single cell. Over the millions of years, in the Precambrian era, the first multicellular or organisms that were made up of more than one cell appear, among them the Trilobites.

With that passing of the years, the species were evolving, adapting to the needs and possibilities offered by their environment, some of them becoming gigantic animals, masters and lords of the land, sea and air, until those species that now are living with us.

This book is not a paleontological, complicated and technical compendium, it aims to tell the story of the exciting search for one of the greatest animals that inhabit our land: the Carcharocles Megalodon, the supreme hunter of the prehistoric seas, a gigantic shark of up to 20 meters long and 30 tons in weight, which was able to swallow a complete whale and that had no difficulty swallowing any dolphin that crossed its path. A fascinating animal that swam in the ancient seas that bathed Peru, probably from the Cretaceous, about 70 million years ago and that had to leave traces somewhere in our country.

No paleontologist doubts that sharks existed much earlier, there is evidence that swam in the seas since the Jurassic era, even some scientists risk ensuring that they already inhabited the land in the Paleozoic, but none of the size and qualities that the king had among sharks, the Megalodon.

In 1972, when I started the passion for fossils, I used to go for a walk with the family of one of my best friends at school, Robert Konopasek, an Austrian who shared the same hobby, inherited from his father geologist. I remember the camps in remote places where we used to bet who found more ammonites. The hobby is maintained until today, taking advantage of the fact that in Europe private extraction and collection is allowed, as long as the specimen found does not exceed a value of 5000 Euros or the place is considered as a study area. It is interesting to note how the European authorities are aware that many of the important findings have been made by amateur paleontologists and opt for a non-prohibitive regulation, which aims to extend the possibilities of finding and maintaining their natural heritage.

Unlike archeology, paleontological remains are brought to the surface by winds, landslides, rivers or some other natural phenomenon and are exposed without mercy to erosion, beginning a rapid process of deterioration that leads to their disappearance in weeks, in some cases such as teeth, even in days.

In September 2007, I decided to take advantage of the visit to Peru of Ingo Meyer, a great friend and collaborator of many German museums, to document the search for Megalodon throughout the country.

The first difficulty we encountered was the lack of paleontological information, we did not find any source of research that gave us an overview of the paleontological distribution of Peru, so we decided to make some trips along the Peruvian coast searching for some vestige that indicated the presence of contemporary animals that could have been the food of the Megalodon. For this, we had to take a tour to different geographical scenarios trying to find fossil vestiges that indicated the paleontological era in which we were moving.

Klaus Hönninger Mitrani

Looking for the Monster: La Libertad, north of Peru

The region of La Libertad, on the north coast of Peru, has a vast desert that extends through the north and south of the city of Trujillo. La Libertad is known worldwide for housing the largest mud citadel in the world, Chan Chan and several of the high Peruvian cultures, among which, without doubt, the Mochica, Chimu and Cupisnique cultures. Apart from the archaeological wealth, the department has a vast area of fossil remains, both on the coast and in the mountains.

We arrived in the city of Trujillo and managed to contact an archaeologist who knew the areas and has been a casual witness, during the years of work in the field, of the presence of fossil remains in the area. One of his casual encounters caught our attention, near a cliff, at the top, he informs us, is the skeleton of a whale. While we are used to finding skeletons of different marine mammals and fish on our beaches, what did a whale skeleton do at 450 meters in the middle of the desert ?

 After renting a 4x4 truck, we started our first trip to that desert area that bears the suggestive name of "Pampa de los Fósiles", very close to the city of San Pedro de Lloc, north of the city of Trujillo. This area is known for its ancient vestiges of the Cupisnique culture and for the stone workshops of the Man of Paiján or also known as the Paijanense Man who inhabited that area 12,000 years ago.

The trip through the Pan American Highway is a special attraction, especially when traveling with foreign visitors, since the reckless maneuvers of some drivers are striking. In fact, our companions were calmer when we entered the

inhospitable desert through an area that didn't show tire tracks or passerby. Through that intact sand, we drived about 11 kilometers to reach the coast, on a journey that required all the car skills to avoid turning in the steep dunes, falling into hidden ravines or getting stuck in the middle of nowhere.

After advancing those 11 kilometers in about 2 hours, we arrived at the place described by our advisor and guide, a mound that showed some bones that he rightly assigned to a whale. Ingo Meyer, the visiting paleontologist confirmed that it was one, but found no comparative trace to determine the era of its origin. In fact, the presence of a fossil whale in that place gave us great hopes of finding some evidence of the presence of sharks, since the whale was his favorite dish.

After touring the surroundings without finding anything, we decided to continue, with a snail's pace.

Ingo Meyer mentioned during the tour, that a whale that has been bitten by a Megalodon is not normally found in the state in which ours was, it is typical to find a sectioned skeleton or simply one of the parts of it.

4 kilometers to the north and having Ingo Meyer in the back of the truck, standing as a sailor looking for land, we  crossed an area that showed, in the distance, a group of bones whitened by the sun, "slowed down to see better - it is a dead horse" - our Trujillo guide told me. I lent myself to follow the path when I hear knocks on the roof of the pickup and shouts of - "Halt" what in german means "stop". We got off the truck and walked towards the bones. Ingo, undoubtedly one of the most famous specialists in his field, indicated to us while we advanced towards the discovery, that those were not horse bones.

The skeletal remains were scattered within a radius of 3 meters, typical distribution for emerging bones that are whipped by the wind. Undoubtedly - Ingo informs us - "these are bones of a tapir from the Holocene era, about 100,000 years old, we are in  the wrong era, we have to go further back into the past."

Although Trujillo left us amazed from its beauty and tourist attractions, we had to undertake the return to Lima to continue the search in the province that assured us the greatest chance of success, the desert of Ocucaje in the region Ica, south of Lima.

Looking for the Monster: Ocucaje, Ica – South of Peru

The city of Ica is located 306 kilometers south of Lima. It was founded with the name of Villa de Valverde, although it was later named San Jerónimo de Ica. It has beautiful covers of colonial haciendas. In its vicinity highlighted the Paracas, Nazca and Chincha cultures. The trip from Lima to Ica by the Panamericana Sur highway, is approximately 4 to 5 hours, depending on the transport.

The city is located on the banks of the Ica River. It irrigates a fertile plain located in the middle of the desert. It is said that the oasis of Huacachina, 5 kilometers from the city, is unique in America. We must point out that in our journey through the inhospitable deserts of Ica, we have found more than one of similar beauty that even served as centers of worship for the ancient cultures of the area.

In the beautiful hotel "El Huarango" we find our guide Néstor Díaz, a stocky man who is not only a broad connoisseur of the deserts of Ica, but also a person with a unique experience in the region.

After the conversation with Néstor Díaz, there was no doubt, we were in the right place. He told us about the remains of large whales and fossilized shark teeth. That is the combination we had been looking for. Ingo Meyer, like the rest of the team, were so fascinated with the anecdotes of Néstor's travels, that we we were impatient to take the course.

Of course, - we were warned - the desert is very dangerous and we must take the necessary measures to avoid suffering any damage. To get to the area in question requires a prepared car and clothing that supports the inclemency of day and night. The temperature can reach, during the day at 45 degrees Celsius (113° Fahrenheit) in the shade and at night at 4 degrees (39° Fahrenheit).

"The desert" – he also warned us – "try to kill you since you enter, it takes away your thirst and hunger, when you realize, you are dehydrated and your pressure drops. A good hat, sunglasses and a special clothing that does not allow the passage of ultraviolet rays, are as essential as an adequate amount of water per person and a balanced meal".

When you talk about the desert, you imagine large areas of sand and dunes that crown a dry and rugged landscape, in fact, a correct but not complete vision, the Ica desert has areas composed of marine sediments that contain calcium carbonate, also known as Limestone, an essential chemical in the production of glass and cement. An intake of this, can cause severe gastric irritation and inhalation causes serious problems in the respiratory system. In addition there are large areas composed of magnesium sulfate, an involuntary intake can cause untreatable diarrhea that would accelerate a dangerous dehydration process.

In fact, the presence of these elements are for an experienced explorer signs of danger that must be faced with proper preparation and equipment. During our trip to the impregnable desert extensions, we would witness the ineffable consequences of an irresponsible and reckless expedition. The trip to so remote and dangerous places can only be organized with guides who know about these

dangers, geography, equipment, safety and contingency measures. An attempt to make an expedition saving these elements is of mortal danger and should not be taken lightly, the desert kills, we are sure of that.

THE EXPEDITION: The adventure begins

The next day, point 6 in the morning, as agreed, our guide appeared and had already conditioned the vehicle, bought the food in sufficient quantities for 4 days, calculating the proportional needs of water and food for the people who made up the expedition, following a pattern that can only be done when you have experience. In the desert you cannot eat or drink anything, you must consider weather factors that influence the digestion and absorption of food and drinks.

After a good breakfast, we set out on the south Pan American Highway, crossing the beautiful valley of Ica.

We went in two cars, but, the "Macho" of Néstor Díaz, a used Jeep that was purchased from the Peruvian army and  extraordinarily conditioned for these hard and dangerous trips, was the best one. Around 8:30 in the morning we arrived at the point of entry to the desert, on the left side you could see the beautiful sedimentary formations, islands that a few million years ago existed in the place. The dryness and infinity of the landscape announced a hard road to our destination.

 The long-awaited time had come to enter the ancient history of the desert of Ica. A strong wind accompanied the request of our guide to hold us well and put on our nose guards to avoid calcium carbonate and magnesium sulfate. Crossing an old hill that housed an old pre-Inca cemetery, which showed signs of looting, we began the uncertain adventure in search of the largest marine giant in the Peruvian Miocene, the Megalodon.

The entrance area was, like everything that is outside the Pan-American Highway, an affirmed route that showed the tracks of some vehicles that enter the surrounding town and the different artisanal mines that abound in the place. A semi-desert landscape with sporadic plantations of chickpeas, beans and palm trees accompanied us in the swing of potholes and mounds. Friendly people raised, in our wake, the hand in greeting. We stopped at a dusty police station to announce our entry into the desert and communicate the return date, which, if not met, was a sign that we had problems, making a search necessary.

One hour from the South Pan American Highway in the west direction, our guide stops to explain the configuration of the land and allow us to rest from the rough road that we had. Sand and first samples of magnesium sulfate were in front of us and separated by a thin border determined by the wind. A short walk not only allowed us to stretch our legs, but it was the first encounter with intense heat typical for the desert areas of these latitudes.

In the following hours, impressive landscapes awaited us with ravines, dunes, dry rivers, lost oases, sedimentary formations, prehistoric beaches that still showed the signs of having been millions of years ago.

But that was not going to be the only thing, we would witness the difficulty of the terrain, the inclement weather and the skill of our guide. It is very difficult to express in words what we have lived to the place chosen for our camp, 5 hours away through one of the driest deserts in the world.

Definitely the entrance to the desert was accompanied by a series of difficulties, although announced, they always cause concern. Soft terrain is almost undetected and those that seems soft, hide carbonate crystals that can cut the tires like sharp knives. The sinking of the jeep was a simple announcement sent to us by the desert, relentless guardian of its treasures.

We were alone trying to quickly release the jeep and not lose time, an entry at noon is usually very dangerous for the engine due to high temperatures and the fine carbonate that adheres to the air filter. After 1 hour of hard work, our guide manages to free the jeep from the sand and we continue towards the top of the plateau, the so-called

"The key", a gully that not anyone dares to cross .

The vision of that gully caused horror, the question reigned among us all - how were they going to go through there? - the soft sand, the climb and a set of rocks formed an impregnable strait. The danger represented by this step, with justice, was baptized as "The key". It was so scary, that we decided to get out of the vehicle, so that our guide could cross it alone. A wise decision since unfortunately we lost one of the vehicles in the attempt to cross into the prehistoric bays. Overcoming the pitfall of "The Key" we saw the majesty of the desert, countless kilometers of bays, islands and strange rock formations. We felt that the exploration journey began from here, we had defeated the guardian and now we could witness what it was hiding from us.

In the distance we could already appreciate the first sedimentary formations.

The way down would prove equally difficult, the sand and bentonite, an organic clay that is formed from the fossilization of the marine plankton, became volcanic ash, the only vestige of some millenary eruption that had swept everything in its path. Our footwear and clothing were quickly impregnated with this fine dust and we should be careful not to breathe it because, as the guide told us, the lungs harden like cement. The tires of our vehicles left deep traces in step raising a dangerous dust that invaded every corner of the vehicle and our bodies.

I felt really happy when we left this stratum and descended to the first great bay that once, millions of years ago, was inhabited by marine animals. From a certain angle, the bay showed us the traces of ancient beaches that were descending as the Andes began to rise, drying them and trapping the animals that inhabited it. A beautiful panorama for the experts present, that were impatient to go down to check the presence of a vestige that leads us to find evidence of the presence of the great prehistoric shark.

With a beautiful view of the bay, we begin to search the area.

A dry river that once brought water to the sea forming a beautiful landscape.

Following the riverbed, we find a beautiful ancient and dry waterfall. Recently a group of journalists who wanted to document this wonder got lost in the desert, for that

reason it has been baptized as "Canyon of the Lost" and so it is now known internationally. Happily the rescue police found the journalists unharmed few hours later.

The wonderful view of the old meandering riverbed and the waterfall curiously breaking the strata, stunned the most tanned of our expeditionaries, nobody had seen this extraordinary formation before. The descent became, in addition to a skill challenge, a box of surprises as we would discover a few minutes later. We already had about 2 hours of travel and we had to hurry down to find a safe place to build our camp. The absolute darkness of the desert is beautiful to let us see a sky adorned by millions of stars and aerosols, but also a dangerous situation, because it

prevents us from distinguishing the deep cliffs. But it is not the only danger, in the afternoon the strong winds ("called Paraca") prevent visibility by raising the fine dust of the desert and quickly irritating the eyes and throat. Our guides assure us that a certain height and the sand dunes pointing north are the best protection for the inclement weather of this place. They would protect us from the wind and the intense cold of the night. Desert connoisseurs know that clothing should protect the body from the sun and heat during the day, another story is that clothing that is required for raw nights with temperatures that, depending on the time, can go down to 5 degrees Celsius (39° Fahrenheit).

The descent to the first bay was long and tedious; cars had to circumvent a series of dangerous slopes that threatened to turn us into the smallest driving error. An accident in such a remote place would represent being at the mercy of the inclement weather, making a return to civilization almost impossible. In fact, having chosen to enter with an expert guide gave us some security but the desert would quickly show us that strict laws that demand the highest knowledge of survival are in their domain; A skeleton in front of us tragically showed us the fate of a person who lost the battle against the rugged, aggressive and inclement nature. An unfortunate finding that confronted us against a series of questions and fears that we had to suppress.

At that time I remembered the words of one of our collaborators who claimed that the desert was a monster that tried to kill you since you stepped on their domains, without a doubt, in front of us was the unfortunate proof of it.

An hour later, we arrived at the area of our camp. Because the wind is very strong, we have to camp protected by a dune. This protected area with dunes also helps us to install the tents and the campfire.

Summer nights, when it's not cold, many of us prefer to sleep without a tent.

If the nights in the desert are indescribable, the sunset is usually even more. The day says goodbye very early showing a changing range of colors, where clouds are responsible for transporting light and shadow in its path. The horizon is capable of showing all the variety of blue and yellow tones highlighted by a matt black that characterizes sedimentary formations. The surrounding rocks acquire a silhouette that in many cases is confused with threatening giants or lurking bandits. The night is so dark that when you leave the campfire you walk as if your eyes were closed. The starry sky invites you to sit watching it waiting for some meteor to break with the immobility of the millions of luminous points. In a single night we came to count 18 meteorites of different sizes and more than one caused a great surprise for its size and wake. The temperature drops drastically making it necessary to shelter as in the coldest European winter. The humidity increases leaving a marked dew on all objects that are at a certain height. Together with darkness, cold and humidity, absolute silence is a notable factor achieving a combination that does not exist when living in a city. Life changes not only for us humans, nocturnal fauna makes its appearance in different ways, a howl of the fox often accompanies a heartbreaking groan of some night bird. In the early morning, the slight footsteps of the fox that surrounds the camp in search of food cause fear in more than one, the fantasy of those present in the

Interpretation of the sounds reaches, in many cases, cinematographic limits.

The first rays of the sun and the climate still mild, invite you to start the first walk to the nearest bay, about two hundred meters from the camp.

A bay is always a good place to start the search for some fossil hint that allows us to determine the geological time in which we find ourselves. When we talk about bay, we mean the one that once was with water that housed fish, mollusks, cetaceans and all the marine fauna that lived at

that time. The uprising of the Andes and the withdrawal of water were the causes of desert formation. In the photo below we can see the elements mentioned, we are standing very close to the shore, in an area that was not very deep and was formerly underwater. In the upper center of the photo we can see where the shore was and in

the background formations representing two islands.

As we approach the shore, we observe the small red "stones". At first we thought that these were concretions, but as we approached we were surprised that they were fossilized mollusks, or rather, their molds.

As in our times, the shore was full of waste, in this case wood that has fossilized.

The discovery of a fossilized shark tooth of the Isurus Hastalis species, better known as Mako, was a sign that the bay had housed this species and that we were in a possible hunting ground for different shark species.

The Mako was a large predator belonging to the Lamnidae family that inhabited the different oceans of the world between 10 and 4 million years. Its size was 6 meters in length and it is estimated that it weighed about 1500 kilos. He was one of the great predators that inhabited the Peruvian coast in the past, only surpassed at that same time, by the Carcharocles Megalodon, our giant. Sharks can only breathe when they are moving, so nature has made them true eating machines. In this process they usually lose teeth that would put their dietary needs at risk if they were not equipped with a mechanism to renew them.

These animals have several rows of replacement teeth that appear at the loss of one.

The shore of the bay had given us the first clue, it was time to go down to what was once the seabed and look for more vestiges of large marine life or rather, that life that was the food of the Megalodon such as whales, dolphins or sea lions.

According to geologists, the desert of Ica was formed at the end of the Secondary era, at the end of the Late Cretaceous, by the subduction movement of the Nazca plate under the South American Plate, thereby creating the Andes and pushing the Sea to the west. Seismic movements and subsequent volcanic activity have been more important in the relief configuration than external erosive agents. The ancient sea shows two types of beach, the first called "protected beach", which were bays with low current or strong waves, is where fossil remains of mollusks and mammals are in good condition, often in a living position . The second is called "agitated beach", here we find fragmented shells and isolated bones.

Our first bay was, due to its configuration and without a doubt, a protected beach.

Descending to the once seabed in search of complete vestiges

First signs, a set of vertebrae and ribs of some marine

mammal, Erosion destroys traces when they appear on the surface. We found also first remains of large mammals, like whale skeletons destroyed by erosion.

Extremely rare finding, part of the whale's crystallized brain

The presence of skeletal remains of large mammals at the bottom of the bay gave us the best conditions to find evidence of the presence of the giant Megalodon, a deep protected beach was an ideal dining room for sharks, as it could stalk its prey with greater ease. Imagine a single entry and exit to the bay, sharks entering it and cornering its prey. The marine life on this beach not only consisted of whales or dolphins, but as the following finding would corroborate us, also of sea lions.

Our companions, experts in determining paleontological ages, confirm that the remains found so far correspond to the Miocene, 24 to 5 million years old, at which time the Megalodon lived.

The state of the remains is unfortunate, erosion does not forgive and a fossil that appears on the surface is destroyed in a few days by the effects of sun and wind. A fact that must be taken into consideration by the authorities that claim to protect the cultural heritage, prohibiting any extraction or removal of fossil remains and preferring their definitive destruction. Paleontology cannot be managed like archeology, here it is not excavated to reach the legacy, fossils appear by the effects of the wind and are destroyed forever. In other countries, smarter measures are taken that allow fossil remains to be rescued even by amateurs as long as they are later reported to the authorities who determine their stay in a museum or exhibition place. Measures like this one could save fossil vestiges of incalculable cultural value.

One of the important things I learn begins with the discovery of the first bones. Our guide confesses that there is a basic rule in the paleontology of the area, where we see bones is because sharks attacked and where they attacked they lost teeth. A rule that would be confirmed very quickly a few centimeters from the remains of the sea lion.

An Isurus hastalis tooth found near the sea lion.

While our experts kept looking for more vestiges that determined the presence of Megalodon in the bay and with it, the possibility of finding their remains, I marched through the area to confirm if the "bone-tooth" rule was real and not a causality.

In the center of the photo, the bone. Up the tooth of Isurus Hastalis, the rule was fulfilled again.

The discovery of a second shark tooth at close range made me presage that this bay had been filled with sharks. In addition to this omen, the fact that this tooth was so close

to a piece of hip bone confirmed the "bone-tooth" rule, without a doubt, the animal to which this hip belonged, had been devoured by a shark of the species Isurus hastalis and what he had left was one of his teeth.

I decide to continue my march through the area, not only with the certainty that the rule was confirmed, but because of the curiosity of discovering another variety of shark.

And here more examples for the rule.

View that normally one has of the ground, only the bone fragments are noted.

Close-up of the previous picture, we can see a shark tooth near the bone destroyed by the sun and wind.

It was really incredible that each bone was accompanied by one or more teeth, in many cases the form of attack and the place of the bite could be reconstructed. Once the rule was well learned, our guide extended it to the fact that the bigger the bone, the bigger the shark that caused the death of the animal. This meant that if we were looking for the largest shark, we should concentrate on the large fossil remains.

I decided to go down to deeper places of the bay in search of whales or dolphins and with impressive success. Before my eyes stood the skeleton of a great whale that seemed to have been split in two, it was necessary to discover if this was the product of erosion or it was the victim of some predator. In the sequence of following photos we can see why my great surprise and emotion.

Now to find out which shark had attacked him, following the theory that they always lost teeth when biting.

And so it was, the killer had left his mark on the remains, a great Isurus Hastalis had attacked this whale !

Teeth embedded in the remains, an orgy of flesh that had left teeth everywhere !

The whale had been attacked by a 6-meter shark with sharp teeth that even, after millions of years, still maintain their sharpness. The decision to visit this bay had become a real genius, a few meters from the shore the vestiges documented the life of the marine fauna of the Miocene era. The finding of the whale killed by the Isurus Hastalis and the embedded teeth were worth their weight in gold in efforts to document the behavior of sharks at that time. It had been attacked very close to the shore, in not very deep waters, which would require a deep analysis.

What caught my attention mightily was the fact that the shark Isurus Hastalis was not the only one that swam at that time, but we did not find evidence of the presence of other species. We decided to keep up with the finding and take a tour

of the hillside in search of teeth that will indicate the presence of other shark species.

On one of the slopes we found what we were looking for, in the same place evidence of the existence of other shark species and with it we confirmed that the different sharks lived together and fed on the same animal. The largest shark attacked and devoured much of the greater prey, the smaller sharks assumed the leftovers. In the case of small prey such as fish, the small shark attacked directly and devoured them. In the sequence of photos below we see the millimeter work of finding the teeth of the smallest sharks.

Many of the species were very small and had to be seen more closely

The discovery, in the vicinity, of different types of shark completed the framework that was required to reconstruct

the fauna of the area, we had found traces of fishes, sea lions, dolphins, whales and their respective predators that went from a small Carcharhinus Brachyurus that It did not pass 1 meter long, to a large Isurus Hastalis of 6 meters. The sequence shows the different species found in the bay that was baptized by our guide as "Klaus Bay" for my enthusiasm in finding traces of small sharks that normally go unnoticed to the human eye, but I think it was more because of being hours kneeling on the floor looking for them.

In this bay we find teeth of different sharks, some with beautiful colors that are due to the minerals that abound such as iron oxides. The inventory was great !

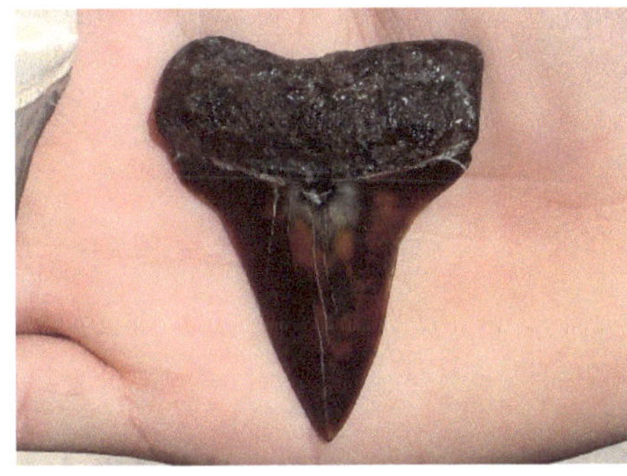

Tooth of Isurus Hastalis. The red color is possibly due to the presence in the fossilization of iron oxide.

Shark tooth of the species Isurus Hastalis, better known as Mako

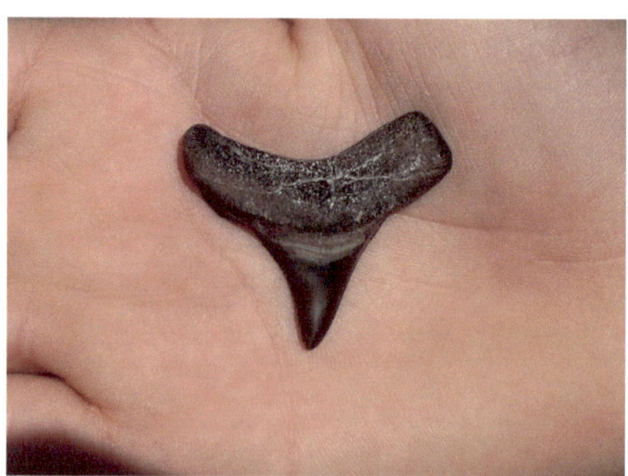

Shark tooth of the species
Carcharhinus leucas.

Shark tooth of the species Isurus Ferox

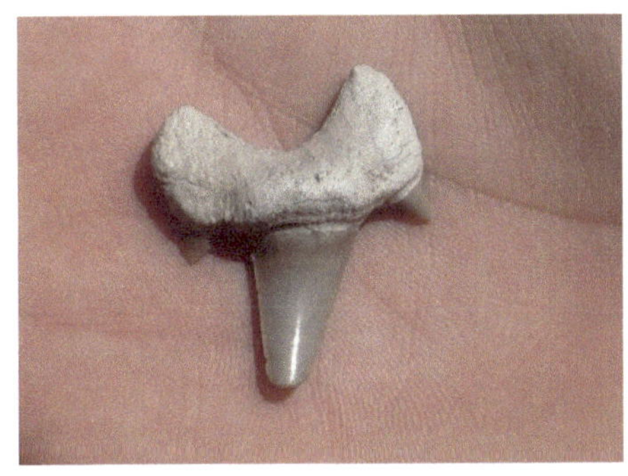

A variant of the Isurus Ferox? Here I was not sure.

Classification is pending

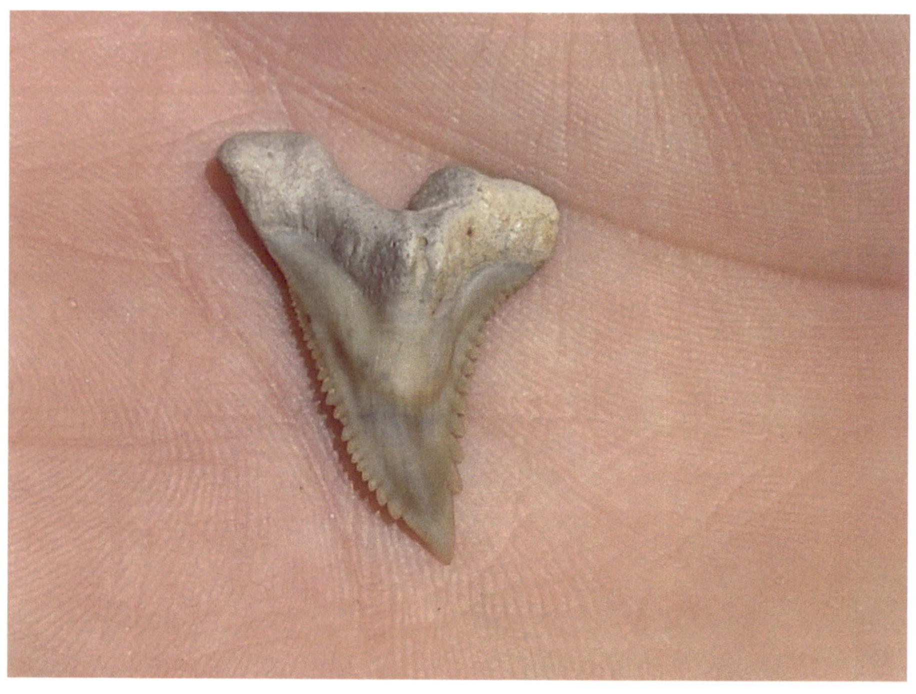

Shark tooth of the species Hemipristis Serra

Strange tooth shape, possibly from a shark Alopias Vulpinus

Shark tooth of the species Galeocerdo Contortus

Shark tooth in the species Carcharhinus leucas

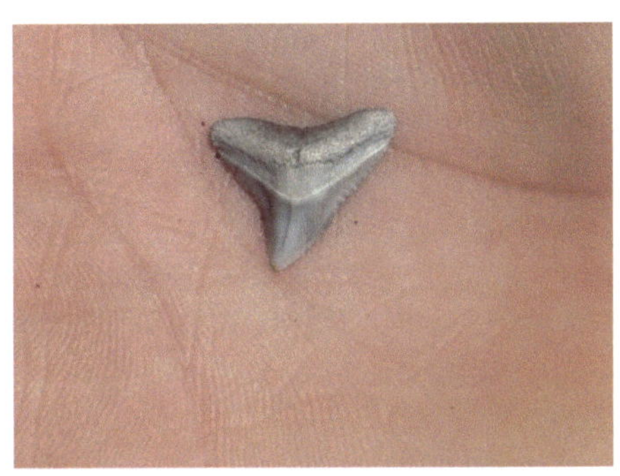

Two teeth that surprised us, above a species to be determined and below that of a Carcharocles Chubutensis, the predecessor of our giant, the Carcharocles Megalodon and from the Hemipristis Serra. The discovery of a small tooth of a shark of the species Carcharocles Chubutensis surprised us since it is the predecessor of the Carcharocles Megalodon, our giant. This finding led us to define the area where we were belongs to an older era and suddenly there were vestiges of more modern ages. We had found Pliocene and Miocene shark teeth in the same bay and at the same segmental height. A well preserved stingray palate was also a surprise.

One of our companions tells us that there are vestiges that the area was at different heights in the different geological ages, this means that it went up and down several times, a fact that would be demonstrated later with the finding in the middle of the bay of an animal that It did not correspond to the place or the era.

Together with the teeth detected and in the middle of a bay full of marine fauna, one of our companions made an incredible discovery, the skeleton of a terrestrial mammal, a Megatherium, it was a huge lazy that inhabited South America since the beginning of the Pliocene (5 to 2.5 million years) until the end of the Pleistocene (2.5 million to 100,000 years). An upright lazy adult reaches 4 meters high and could exceed 4,000 kilos. Remains with 6 meters in length have been found in Argentina. It is claimed that the Megatherium were herbivores. The characteristics of the teeth and the remains of excrement recently found in different parts of America, support this theory.

Fossil remains of the Megatherium, rolled !

The depth of the bay had not yet opened all its secrets to us, the more we advanced or descended, the greater were the beautiful vestiges that appeared before our eyes. One of them caught my attention, it was the complete skeleton of a bearded whale, that instead of teeth, it has a beard, it measures about 12 meters in length, which rests like a historical monument crying out for its preservation. A paleontological beauty threatened by wind and sun that must be urgently preserved before it disappears forever. Remains like this are not found anywhere in the world.

Close-up of the beard

The diversity of fossil remains was overwhelming, very interesting for both geologists and paleontologists who continued their work while we, curious amateurs, walked through the place  ecstatic with the emotion of shouting the discovery of something extraordinary. One of the things that caught my attention was the presence of conglomerates of earth that appeared to be lumps of different sizes and that looked like a hardened mud. In one of them I could appreciate the presence of a bone, which led me to consult the experts who had traveled with us. I learned that they are locked with organogenic rocks that are called "concretions" in geology. Organogenic rocks, are formed with remains of living beings. The most abundant have been formed with skeletons as a result of biomineralization processes; some, however, have been formed by the evolution of organic parts (of cellular matter), and are properly called organic rocks. Concretions in general usually form during diagenesis (it includes the processes that a sediment undergoes until it becomes a rock). In it the organism that has been buried acts as a cement core around which the mineral grains are cemented.

Other concretions such as those of the fish of the Santana Formation of Brazil are generated in the environment where the animal lived. Thus these fish lived in ponds, in a dry environment, in which these ponds were often seasonally dried and then the fish are a wrapped by the sediment. We found a lot of fishes and other remains inside.

An esplanade full of concretions, without exaggeration, thousands!

Concretion with a fish, we found hundreds of them

Concretion with almost a complete head of a dolphin

While the mark of a Megalodon tooth in a concretion would be nothing spectacular for an inexperienced, if it was for those who were looking for proof of their presence in this bay. When an animal found a hunting ground rich in wildlife, it generally remained or returned to it until death. It was time to follow up on our giant and search every corner. A second finding of a concretion within a few minutes increased the expectation and indicated that we were in the correct stratum. For those readers who do not know these terms, in geology each layer of sediment is presented as stratum.

The thickness of a sediment allows to deduce the time it took to form, if the sedimentation rate is known. Each type of sediment indicates some characteristics of the time in which it was formed, such as rains, glaciations, desertification, etc. All this allows geologists to know the age of the sediment and, therefore, also the age of the fossils it contains, resulting in a good dating method.

It seems that fate was leading us a little towards what we were looking for, each finding of a vestige of the giant increased with the passage of time. Although the following finding can only be attributed to a wind transport of the finding, this means by wind action. The tooth found by one of our companions, who until that day was dedicated to being a housewife, contravened all logic. Anecdotally, your search in that stratum was taken by one of our guides as an example of the knowledge that only a housewife could apply.

The root of a Megalodon tooth sticking out, the deterioration due to erosion is already noticeable.

The finding of this tooth was extremely didactic, for two main reasons, the first demonstrated the effects of erosion: the root that appeared was already in the process of deterioration due to the sun and wind, the rest was covered by the thin layer of diatomite and, therefore, intact despite the passage of millions of years. Diatomite is a silica rock of sedimentary origin, presenting varying degrees of consolidation; It is mainly made up of fossilized diatomaceous remains. Diatoms are photosynthetic organisms that are part of the plankton (phytoplankton). They have an olive gold color, due to

their different photosynthetic pigments. The second because the tooth was in a place where it should not be, this demonstrated the theory of wind displacement (eolic), the stratum where it should be, was tens of meters higher. The wind had eroded the stratum and rolled parts of it downhill, including fossils. A far-fetched theory if it had not been because very close there we found the reliable proof of it, another Megalodon tooth lay, in the middle of the slope, as if someone had put it for the picture. It was evident that he had recently rolled from the upper stratum and was stuck in a small rock.

Megalodon tooth that had rolled from the upper stratum, with part of a whale bone

This displacement due to the effect of the wind is not only in both cases seen above, we have had the opportunity to find different types of vestiges in the middle of nowhere or at the base of the slopes, where the inexperienced would think they were put by someone to impress the visitor.

Tooth of Isurus hastalis displaced by the wind and embedded in the ground

We had mentioned at the beginning of this book that desert fossils appear due to erosion. These have been hidden for millions of years under layers of sediment, which have served as protection for fragile petrified remains. Many readers will be surprised to hear about the fragility of a petrification, but it really is. We had also mentioned about the destruction caused by the sun and winds, in the following photos we will see some examples of the state in which some teeth after remaining 2 or 3 days exposed, but first we must understand the way it happens.

Typical are the expansion cracks due to the effects of the sun, in a few days these fissures will cause the tooth to split into several pieces that will be scattered by the wind and will disappear without a trace !

It all starts with fissures and then the tooth "explodes" practically !

Typical example, the tooth was broken by the effects of heat, the other half was scattered by the wind

Sometimes, when one arrives on time, it is possible to find a tooth that has not yet been destroyed and can be repaired.

Tooth of Carcharocles Chubutensis destroyed by the sun and the wind, but still salvageable.

It would have been a shame to miss this beautiful tooth forever.

But not only teeth are destroyed, dolphin fossil totally splintered by erosion, a vestige lost forever.

Undoubtedly, the bay we had chosen for the search was full of vestiges and surprises, but it was also very exposed to the sun and wind. We had to be very lucky to find our giant since, as we saw, we had to be in the right place at the right time, anticipating erosion or begging for the skeleton to appear during the night, so that we find it before destroy. But that was not the whole problem, unlike bone fossils, the internal skeleton of sharks rarely petrifics since it is made up of cartilage, which is why the fossil record of sharks is usually made up of isolated teeth. The possibility of finding one was supported only by the fact that Nestor Diaz Zegarra had found in this desert, some years ago, a fossilized skeleton of an Isurus Hastalis, possibly an adult specimen that had fallen into deep water thus preventing its destruction or that He had absorbed the surrounding calcium carbonate during his fossilization.

Using our experience, we decided to move to a nearby bay that was protected from the sun and wind. The characteristics were similar and were interconnected by a wide channel that allowed us to suspect that sharks visited it with the same frequency. Like everything that happened until that moment, the road had several surprises. Our accompanying geologist noticed something strange on one of the slopes and asked us to stop to check it. It was a meteorite impact that had compressed several strata.

The surrounding bay was just on the other side of the hillside that showed a possible meteorite impact, which is why Nestor Diaz and the author decided to look for some vestige of the celestial body. The possibility of finding something was very remote since meteorites are often pulverized in the impact, but rookie curiosity was stronger than logic. We check the surroundings to find an area with impactite, evidence of high temperature and shock metamorphism of some object.

Néstor Díaz standing on the impactite, classic material of impact of some object, notice above the crater filled with sand and mineral dust.

The geological studies carried out during the last decades have shown us that our planet has been subjected to a meteoric bombardment similar to that suffered by the Moon, and even more intense. In fact, due to its greater force of gravity, the impact rate on Earth is 1.5 times higher than that of our natural satellite. Although researchers have found a good number of impact craters on the earth's surface, the total amount of these is apparently low, which can be easily explained due to the fact that geological activity has been erasing them over millions of years. Some causes can be invoked that explain the "disappearance" of these impact structures such as erosion (especially old craters and mainly those of small diameter) or are hidden, covered by volcanic or sedimentary materials, only detectable as geophysical anomalies. Tectonic activity also plays an important role, they may have deformed them, so that they are unrecognizable.

There is also, among all known impact structures, a "deficit" of craters with small diameters (less than 20 km), which are easier to erase from the earth's surface than large ones. So this finding was very interesting. In Peru, only one recorded impact is known, that of Tambo Quemado in Ayacucho of 1950. The meteorite dropped in Puno has not yet been studied or analyzed for what is not yet considered as an official record. Logic told us that if the meteorite had survived the impact, it should have bounced back towards the bay, so we decided to review the environment. It was not long until we found a suspicious rock that differed from those of the place.

Strange stones very close to the place of impact, showed signs of heat fusion, which led to suspicion that it was a meteorite.

A few meters away were two smaller ones that also showed signs of high temperature melting, which made these three stones clear suspects of being a meteorite.

The author sent a small fragment to the Max Planck Institute in Germany to analyze with positive results. It was a meteorite of the type Chondrite H4 W3 and that has been registered in the International Meteorite Society under the name of "Cerro La Tiza" with code 44877, being this the second found in Peru.

While this unsuspected finding had moved us emotionally away from the main search, we met with the group to continue the work of finding the remains of the Megalodon.

The first thing that came before us was an immense tooth of Megalodon that welcomed us or, who knows, the farewell. His condition was unfortunate, but it reminded us that we were leaving the bay exposed to look for a protected one. The amount of Megalodon tooth remains

had increased substantially with the advance into deeper areas, which made us think that we were entering the territory of one or more Megalodons. Another important factor was the fact that we had not found any whole whale or other large animal, we had encountered skeletons that rather had the appearance of having been bitten. A half whale indicated the way forward. In the distance we could see another whale.

Following the extraordinary path, we found an unusual vestige for the place, a very old obsidian knife. The guide explains that the ancient fishermen of the ancient Paracas or Nazca culture (700 BC – 700 AC) walked through these places, without a doubt, one of them had lost one of his important tools on the way to the sea.

Again an unexpected finding that could not take us away from our purpose, it was important to continue our way to a protected bay. As I said, experience had taught us that if we wanted to find fossils without damage or with very little, we should look in those bays protected from the wind.

In that new protected bay, the frequency of Megalodon's tooth findings confirmed that we were in a place frequented by this giant. The protected bay kept the remains in good condition and gave us the opportunity to interpret what life had been like in this place millions of years ago. Whales, dolphins, sea lions, penguins and fishes of all sizes had

inhabited it. The presence of small shark teeth such as Carcharinus or Galeocerdo confirmed our theory that this bay had housed predators of different sizes. The remains of mammals with the presence of teeth of several sharks also confirmed that the food chain began with the large ones and that the small ones fed on the remains left by them.

The enthusiasm was greater when our guide called us raising his thumb as a sign of success. Very close to the shore of a beach we could see him kneeling very close to a mound, sketching a smile that mixed with a look of pride. He had found a skeleton of a great shark, an Isurus Hastalis in a spectacular state. While they were not the remains of our giant, experts knew that this finding could bring us closer to the Megalodon.

In all cases where we find Isurus hastalis teeth, we also find Megalodon teeth. That makes us assume that the biggest sharks of that era hunted in the same deep bays.

Part of the spine of an Isurus hastalis and a conglomerate of teeth were exposed

While we were documenting the finding and the corresponding measurements were made, our guide continued with his walk around the beach. The experts had assured us that the Isurus Hastalis found and its condition, increased the possibility of finding a greater vestige of the Megalodon. It hadn't been 10 minutes when we heard screams of "here it is - here it is" causing us to run to the place. We stood a short distance as if by superior order, perhaps looking for the face that showed the greatest surprise. Before our eyes was the spine, at the foot of a mound, of a great shark. A conglomerate of scattered brown objects made us suspect that it could be the teeth of a Megalodon.

Although the vertebrae were very large, in the distance it was not possible to determine what type of shark it was. Crouched by the mound, Nestor Diaz points out some protruding teeth, there was no doubt, they were Megalodon's teeth. The surprise would be even greater when at the top of the mound we found the rest of the teeth exposed, it was our giant looking imposing even millions of years after his death.

When we thought that was all, on the right side of the mound, the jaw of the giant we were looking for, was seen in the sediment ! We had achieved the feat of finding the giant almost complete, the Megalodon !

Gradually cleaning the top of the mound, the spine and jaw appeared.

The finding of this Megalodon constitutes a worldwide sensation. While much of the jaw had disappeared, the nearly 18-meter skeleton of one of the largest predators that furrowed the seas of the Peruvian coast, is a gem for paleontology.

This great fossil has been protected so that it is not destroyed by erosion and has been hidden in the place of the discovery until the necessary coordination with the authorities is made for its legal extraction, preparation and exposure to the national and foreign public. The group has been trying to obtain the necessary funds for the donation of a paleontological museum that houses the wonders that history still hides.

The author also wants to emphasize the fact that there are people in the country who say they represent an authority or museum that has been caught in fraganti extracting fossils with foreign collectors and merchants. The natural heritage of the nation must be adequately protected and if the state represented by the Culture Ministry does not have the funds or specialized personnel, it must allow the private initiative to support without bureaucratic or legal obstacles.

We must be aware that Peru has a wealth that goes beyond archeology, is considered abroad as one of the countries with the largest fossil remains on the planet and this could represent a magnet for a type of tourism that is not yet being exploited . The desert of Ica abandoned by its aridity can generate unsuspected income for the region, it is a piece of unused productive land that must take its place in tourist and scientific importance.

I urge the authorities to contribute to the realization of the museum that Peru requires and not to close the door for those who try to attract private investment in a sector that is not contemplated by the nation's budget.

The giant Megalodon needs its seat in Peruvian history !

But before finalizing this book, I want to make it clear that the desert of the Ica region in Peru should be considered the largest paleontological cemetery of marine vertebrates in the world that must be protected from miners, car races like de Rally Dakar and other activities that in recent years have destroyed important vestiges.

Fossils are not just stones, they are evidence of past life that show us evolution, extinction and can teach us the importance of the environment.

The soil of the desert of Ica with the concetración of minerals such as silica have made it possible, even, that we find fossils of 40 million years with preserved skin.

The care of this paleontological wonder is the obligation of all humanity!